# I CAN BE A
# TEXTILE WORKER

By Christine Maloney Fitz-Gerald

Prepared under the direction of Robert Hillerich, Ph.D.

CHILDRENS PRESS®

CHICAGO

Library of Congress Cataloging in Publication Data

Fitz-Gerald, Christine Maloney.
  I can be a textile worker.

  Includes index.
  Summary: Discusses the people who work with textiles
and clothing, including designers, factory workers
involved in weaving and spinning, dyers, and finishers.
  1. Clothing workers—Juvenile literature.
2. Textile workers—Juvenile literature. [1. Textile workers.
2. Clothing workers.   3. Occupations]
I. Title.
HD8039.C6F57   1987      677'.0023'73     87-10716
ISBN 0-516-01912-0

Childrens Press®, Chicago
Copyright ©1987 by Regensteiner Publishing Enterprises, Inc.
All rights reserved. Published simultaneously in Canada.
Printed in the United States of America.
1 2 3 4 5 6 7 8 9 10 R 96 95 94 93 92 91 90 89 88

# PICTURE DICTIONARY

clothes

costume

wool

cotton

sketch

fabric

synthetic

textile designer

studio

loom

dyer

warp threads

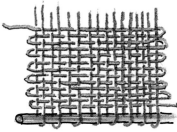
weft threads

plain weave

stylist

portfolio

gamp

Clothes keep us warm in winter and cool in summer. Colors make clothes more interesting.

Clothes keep us warm in winter. They protect us from the sun's rays in summer. But clothes do much more than this.

Our clothes tell other people about ourselves. Clothes can make us seem happy or sad, serious or funny, bold or shy. By looking at the clothes we wear, people can guess whether we're

clothes

The clothes people wear on stage (above) are called costumes.
The clothes people wear for special work are often called uniforms.
Paramedics (right) wear uniforms when they work.

costume

going to school, on
vacation, or to work.
Clothes can even tell
other people about the
work we do.

Actors and actresses
use costumes to tell us
more about the people
they are playing.

Most people wear their favorite clothes when they are not working.

Most of us have a favorite outfit. We wear it again and again. Even when it's old, we don't want to part with it. It feels right and we are comfortable with what it says about us.

7

Male and female models show off the clothes the designer makes.

Even the shape and
style of our clothes give
clues about us. So does
the way we wear our
clothes. The color and
texture in the cloth send
a message, too.

Designers draw the designs and
pick the colors for the cloth.

sketch

textile designer

Many different people
make the cloth, or textiles,
we use. Textile designers
draw the design for the
cloth. They want their
ideas to become

9

All of these different
fabrics were
designed by someone.

beautiful and useful
fabrics that people will
want for their clothes and
many other things around
them.

fabric

Designers are artists.
Most textile designers
have a college degree in
fine arts. They have a
good sense of color. They
know about different
types of fibers.

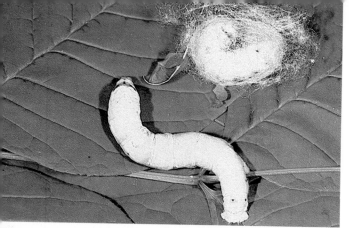

Silk is made by the silkworm (top left). Wool comes from sheep (left) and cotton (above) comes from the cotton plant.

wool

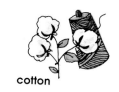
cotton

synthetic

All cloth starts with tiny fibers. Some fibers, such as wool, are from animals. Others, such as cotton, are from plants. Many others, called synthetics, are man-made.

Designers get some ideas from nature. A shell, feathers, flowering plants, or a starry sky could give a designer a plan. Man-made things—skyscrapers, bridges, or factory machinery—can also spark an idea. Museums, art galleries, and the theater are good places to look for design ideas.

sketch

studio

Most designers work in studios. If the designer works for a large textile or design company, the studio may be a large, busy, noisy room. Some designers work for themselves and may have a small home studio.

Designers make sketches of their ideas, using chalk, paint, or even pieces of paper.

Today many designers plan their designs on computers.

They must think about how the fabric will be used. They try different colors. They work with different fabrics—silk, cotton, wool, or synthetic. Some designers use computers to help them.

Designers work on sketches until they are happy with them. A designer who works for a company takes a final sketch to the design director. The director will either accept or reject the design.

portfolio

Designers who work for themselves have a harder job. They must take their portfolios to different companies, trying to sell

A designer (right) works on a pattern. The painted design (left) was
used to make a pattern that is coded to work on an automatic loom.

their designs. Free-lance
designers must communicate
well. A good presentation
helps to sell work.

Designers are happy
when their work is bought

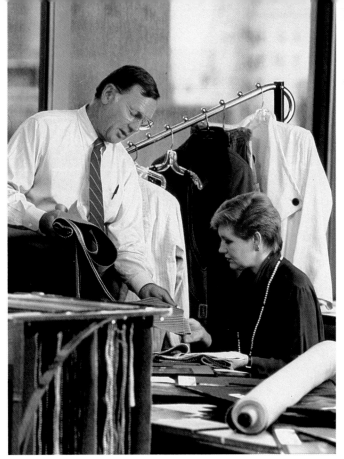

After the cloth has been designed, sales people sell it to the customer.

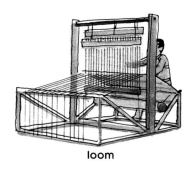
loom

or accepted. However, it will take months for their designs to be made into cloth.

Most cloth is woven on looms in factories. Some cloth is knit, not woven.

Looms are used to weave cloth. Some looms are operated by hand (left). Others work automatically.

Weaving is the criss-crossing of yarns. Some yarn, called warp threads, is attached to the loom. Warp threads run the length of cloth. Weft, or woof, threads run

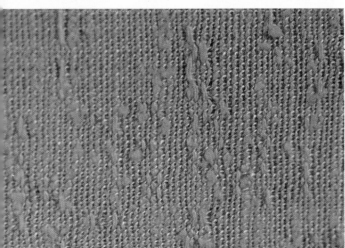

The plaid wool (top left) and linen cloth (left) were woven by machine. The Moroccan woman (above) is weaving a rug by hand.

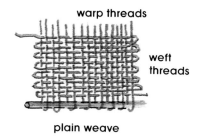

warp threads

weft threads

plain weave

from side to side. They are woven under or over the warp threads. In plain weave, the simplest pattern, the weft thread goes over one warp thread and under the

Looms in a textile factory in Virginia.

next. Looms are set to
control which warp
threads are picked up
each time a weft thread
is passed back and forth.
Looms can weave many
complicated patterns.

Many people work hard to make textiles. Yarn must be spun from fibers. Yarn for the warp must be measured and cut. The warp must be set up on the loom. All of this work is done by powerful machines. Machine operators run the machinery. They must be skilled and alert.

Few people still spin yarn by hand (top left). Most
yarn is spun by machine in factories.

Technicians operate the automatic looms used in factories.

Technicians keep the machines in good working order. Some operators and technicians work at night because textile plants run around the clock.

Yarns and threads are dyed in huge machines.

Workers called dyers
color the cloth or yarns.
They must know about
different types of dyes
and fibers. They use
computers to help match
colors.

dyer

Woman (left) weaves silk cloth by hand in Thailand. Beautiful patterns, such as those shown on these Japanese sashes (above), can be woven by hand or by machine.

gamp

stylist

At first, only a small cloth sample is woven. It is called a gamp. The gamp is sent to the stylist who decides on any final changes in color, texture, or pattern. The stylist also gives the textile a name.

The denim cloth for your favorite blue jeans is woven by machine.

Now the looms weave the textile on huge machines. After weaving, the cloth goes to the finishers. The finishers process the cloth to give it special qualities. It may need to be heat-resistant or waterproof. Finishers

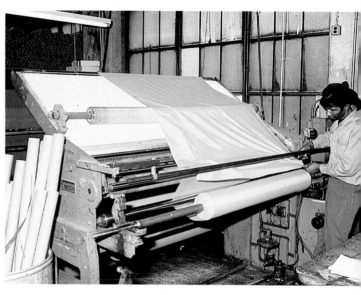

Workers inspect the fabrics before they are shipped to customers.

know how to treat fabric to give it the qualities it needs.

The finished cloth is wound in large rolls and sent to showrooms. It is ready for sale.

Clothing, whether fancy or plain, is made from
fabric that started out as an idea in a designer's head.

The fabric for these
clothes started as an idea
in the mind of a designer.
It took the hard work and
talents of many people to
take that idea and turn it
into a beautiful fabric.

## WORDS YOU SHOULD KNOW

**accept** (ack • SEPT)—to take gladly; receive

**alert** (ah • LERT)—attentive, watchful

**communicate** (kuh • MYOON • ih • kait)—exchange thoughts or ideas through speech, writing, or signals

**cotton** (KAHT • in)—soft white fibers attached to seeds of the cotton plant, collected and drawn into threads or yarn for weaving into cloth

**criss-cross** (KRISS • KROSS)—marked with lines that cross one another

**degree** (dih • GREE)—a title earned from a college or university upon completing study in a particular course

**designer** (dih • ZINE • er)—person who creates a plan through drawings or sketches, to be used for a finished purpose, such as making clothing

**fabric** (FAB • rick)—cloth used in making garments or household items

**factory** (FAK • ter • ee)—building in which goods are produced and put together

**fibers** (FYE • berz)—hairlike coverings attached to certain plant seeds, used in making thread and yarn

**free-lance** (FREE lanss)—a person who performs work for others, having no single employer

**galleries** (GAL • er • eez)—buildings or rooms that display art objects, paintings, sculpture, for public view, or for sale

**guess** (GESS)—to suppose without having certain or complete knowledge

**looms** (LOOMZ)—machines on which yarns or threads are arranged and woven to produce fabric

**portfolio** (port • FOLE • ee • oh)—a set of drawings or designs bound in book form, or carried loose in a folder

**process** (prah • sess)—a system of actions or changes for producing a desired result

**sketches** (SKETCHIS)—artist's incomplete, rough drawings for testing ideas

**studio** (STOO • dee • o)—a workroom for artists, usually large, with high ceiling and many windows.

**technician** (teck • NISH • in)—person who operates equipment that requires special training

**texture** (TEXT • shur)—the appearance and feel of cloth that results from the arrangement of the thread pattern

**theater** (THEE • ah • ter)—a place where dramatic events take place, having a stage for the actors and seats for the audience

# INDEX

# PHOTO CREDITS

## ABOUT THE AUTHOR

Christine Fitz-Gerald has a B.A. in English Literature from Ohio University and a Masters in Management from Northwestern University. She has been employed by the Quaker Oats Co. and by General Mills. Most recently, she was a strategic planner for a division of Honeywell, Inc. in Minneapolis. She now resides in Chicago with her husband and two young children.